The Book of
Stock Car Wisdom

The Book of
Stock Car Wisdom

Common Sense and Uncommon Genius
From 101 Stock Car Greats

Compiled and Edited by Criswell Freeman

WALNUT GROVE PRESS
Nashville, TN
(615) 256-8584

ISBN 1-887655-12-3

The ideas expressed in this book are not, in all cases, exact quotations, as some have been edited for clarity and brevity. In all cases, the author has attempted to maintain the speaker's original intent. In some cases, material for this book was obtained from secondary sources, primarily print media. While every effort was made to ensure the accuracy of these sources, the accuracy cannot be guaranteed. For additions, deletions, corrections or clarifications in future editions of this text, please write WALNUT GROVE PRESS.

Printed in the United States of America

Book Design by Armour&Armour
Cover Design by Mary Mazer
Typesetting & Page Layout by Sue Gerdes
Edited by Alan Ross and Angela Beasley
4 5 6 7 8 9 10 •   99 00 01

ACKNOWLEDGMENTS .
The author gratefully acknowledges the helpful support and research assistance of Betty Carlan, Karol Cooper, Larry Prince and Alan Ross.

The author also acknowledges special appreciation to the entire staff of the McCaig-Wellborn International Motorsports Research Library at the International Motorsports Hall of Fame at Talladega, Alabama.

To Betty L. Carlan

Friend, Fan, Historian

Table of Contents

Introduction

Stock car racing is more than a sport, it's a way of life. From humble beginnings in the rural South, racing has grown, in a single generation, into something as big as Talladega and as wild as Curtis Turner.

Fans don't just attend races, they organize their lives around them. Sponsors gladly pay millions for the privilege of painting a single car. Drivers no longer run whiskey to pay the bills, they make personal appearances. Many things have changed since the rough-and-tumble days of Fireball Roberts and Joe Weatherly, but one thing remains unchanged: the wisdom of the track.

Stock car racers live with the constant reminder that serious injury, even death, may be waiting quietly in the next turn. Many of the sport's greatest drivers never reach old age. Others suffer debilitating injuries. Racing demands courage and gives perspective. It is no surprise that drivers, crews and fans become philosophical.

This book documents the wisdom, determination and humor of racing's greatest legends. You will find quotations from men named Petty, Earnhardt, Allison, and Waltrip. You will enjoy sayings from champions like Junior Johnson, Alan Kulwicki and Neil Bonnett. You will discover words of hope, persistence and courage because that's what it takes to become a winner.

The simple lessons in this book teach us about racing *and* about life; that's what makes these lessons so important. Because each of us, in our own way, is still waiting for the next green flag to drop.

1

Life

Life, like racing, is unpredictable. One week, you're in the winner's circle, next week, you're into the wall.

Bobby Allison once observed, "I've had more peaks and valleys than the state of Arizona." Bobby could have been speaking for all of us. Each human life has a healthy helping of victories and defeats. It's our job to face them with courage and hope. That's racing. And that's life.

Racing is like life.
If you get up one more
time than you fall,
you'll make it through.

Alan Kulwicki

You can live life well or just live. And the person who makes that decision is you.

Bobby Allison

To really live, you have to live with yourself.

A. J. Foyt

The good Lord doesn't tell you what His plan is, so all you can do is get up in the morning and see what happens next.

Richard Petty

The pressure is there whether you're
in front or behind.

Dale Earnhardt

In every aspect of life, have a game plan,
and then do your best to achieve it.

Alan Kulwicki

Don't ever be afraid to laugh at yourself.
Life is wonderful when you've got
a smile on your face.

Benny Parsons

Life begins at 51.

Harry Gant

Focus on others, not on yourself.
If you focus on yourself all of the time, you
can feel sorry for yourself very quickly.

Elisa Allison
Widow of Clifford Allison

I realized I better enjoy and appreciate and
contribute as much as I can today because
all of this could be gone tomorrow.

Davey Allison
After watching replays of his horrifying Pocono crash

You've got to love this life. And I do.

J.D. McDuffie

You can overcome
anything in the
world but fate.

Richard Petty

I figure you get out of life
just about what
you put into it.

Lee Petty

2

Old-Time Racing

Old-time racing was a rough, tough, door-banging affair. The tracks were dirt, the equipment was primitive, and the purses were tiny. Some of the early stars were reformed whiskey runners. Others were garage owners and mechanics. They came from many different backgrounds, but they all shared a common love of fast cars. Still, rivalries were not always friendly. With no corporate sponsors to offend, drivers were free to drink, cuss and fight, which they did with some regularity.

Today's stars are corporate spokesmen. They must be media conscious, always on good behavior. But once the green flag falls, the best drivers still indulge in a little old-time racing. Thank goodness.

Whiskey runners took pride in fast cars
and driving ability. This naturally
led to competition.

Jerry Bledsoe

In the old days, you had to be more
than good. You had to be good and tough.

Richard Petty

Almost every family that lived close by
made moonshine. It was the only way
we had of making money.

Junior Johnson

Some ol' state trooper chased me thirty-nine times, but he never came close.

Curtis Turner

I got caught at the still – never on the road. They never outrun me.

Junior Johnson

In the early days, not all the drivers were moonshiners, but they all had that same devil-may-care moonshiner's attitude.

Richard Petty

Old-Time Racing

Racin' used to be rough.
Today it's cleaned up a lot. Fans and drivers –
we're all a better class of people.

Richard Petty

In the early days, they'd just as soon fight
as drive. They'd even stop the race and fight.

Junior Johnson

When I first started racing, you didn't dare
bring your wife or girlfriend to the race,
because half the people were drunk
and the rest were fighting.

Richard Petty

I never got hit by a tire iron, but when I hit
somebody with my fist,
they thought it was a tire iron.

Maurice Petty

Down South, drivers were brought
        up at 10 or 11 years old to learn
            how to drive a car.

Fred Lorenzen

Earnhardt has one style – all out and
hard chargin'. It comes from the old days, from
    guys like Junior Johnson and Curtis Turner.
            Years ago there were 10 or 15 guys
            driving that way. Now there's Dale.

Richard Childress

I'm patterned from the old drivers.
    All those guys I watched racing growing up
        were tough old boys. That's where I get
            my aggressive, hard style.

Dale Earnhardt

I guess the country needed the wildness
    of stock car racing – I know the South did.

Richard Petty

Tim Flock would drive in a race
　　with a monkey. His brother Fonty ran
　　Darlington in shorts and a T-shirt.

Ralph Moody

I would like to see Weatherly, Fireball and
　　some of those boys in their prime driving
　　these cars today. You'd be surprised.

Bud Moore

The biggest show that you could ever see
was between Joe Weatherly and Curtis Turner.
It was amazing how they could slide a car
through a corner on a dirt track, side-by-side,
not touching one another and still getting
on with the program. They were great.

Bud Moore

The only thing better than watching
　　Curtis Turner party was watching Curtis
　　Turner drive. He was a natural at both.

Cale Yarborough

When he came home from a race and
there wasn't much dirt on the car, I knew
Daddy probably had won.

Dale Earnhardt

People tell me Daddy was one of the best
ever to slide a car around a dirt short track.

Dale Earnhardt

I knew Daddy was getting serious when he
stopped driving the race car to the tracks.
He towed it on the ground behind the Dodge.
That way, if his car got beat up,
we still had a way home.

Richard Petty

Red clay is the greatest natural
racing surface in the world.

Cale Yarborough

Early on, the cars were getting
faster and faster. And with good reason:
Everybody was cheating.

Richard Petty

We went through the south turn,
turned left, and I started hitting sea gulls.
It sounded like popcorn. I must have hit
75 gulls – it was snowing birds.

Tim Flock

Describing action at Daytona Beach in 1955

When he took that checkered flag, he'd run
the whole race on one set of tires; he was out
of gas, and he had 18 cents in his pocket.
It was incredible.

Wanda Lund Early

Describing Tiny Lund's 1963 Daytona 500 victory

It was easier to make up laps in the old days.
I would hate to have to make a lap up
on a road course.

Rusty Wallace

I had a one-car garage on the end
of my house, and I built my car under
a shade tree. I built it for $400
and had a racing budget of $1,000.

Richard Childress

We'd sleep in the truck and live on
what we won. If we didn't win, we didn't eat.
That's pressure. But we were young, the
racing was great, and man, was it fun.

Bobby Allison

My driving style? I had to drive
according to my pocketbook.

Cecil Gordon

Our first car was number 50 because we paid 50 dollars for it.

Leonard Wood

3
The Drivers

Drivers are a breed apart. Ken Squier observed, "The stock car driver is the new American cowboy." Like gunfighters at a showdown, racers face danger with a calm resignation that leaves the rest of us in awe. When racing luck turns bad, there is remarkably little bitterness.

On the occasion of Joe Weatherly's death, Curtis Turner commented, "There's 400 ways that Joe could have made a rich living, but I don't guess he'd have been happy doing anything else." Turner spoke not just for Weatherly but for drivers everywhere. Our new American cowboys, like their Western counterparts, love their work.

Curtis Turner was the greatest race driver
I ever saw.

Bill France, Sr.

Joe Weatherly was a show-type person.
Spectators loved him. He was a colorful
crowd pleaser – one of a kind.

Banjo Matthews

Fireball Roberts was the most respected
driver there ever was or ever will be.

Ned Jarrett

My greatest racing heroes were
Fireball Roberts and Cotton Owens.

David Pearson

Lee Roy Yarbrough wasn't on top long,
but he could have been.

Cale Yarborough

I don't know of anybody who had more car
control on a half-mile track than Tiny Lund.
He just out-muscled the car. He was
so aggressive, he'd hit you
15 times in one corner.

Buddy Baker

I hope that when 1993 is over, the people
at Winston, the people at NASCAR, and the
competitors will all look back and say,
"We were proud to have him
represent us as our champion."

Alan Kulwicki

From his 1992 Championship Award speech.

Davey Allison was a heck of a tough
competitor, a good friend and a great racer.

Dale Earnhardt

Davey Allison was a blessing.

Eli Gold

The Drivers

If Marty Robbins ever decided to give up
singing and run that car full time,
all of us would have to beware.

Bobby Isaac

I set my mind on one goal:
to be the best there ever was.

Lee Roy Yarbrough

Tim Richmond was a natural.

Harry Hyde

I wanted to do something different.

Alan Kulwicki

On driving a victory lap in the opposite direction after winning his
first NASCAR race. The Polish victory lap became his trademark.

I make a lousy spectator.

Neil Bonnett

Speed?
I wouldn't mind if we drove this car
250 miles per hour. My bass boat
goes faster than 100, and I'm thinking
about putting a second motor on it.

Neil Bonnett

I guess Bobby Allison told Neil Bonnett that
there was one requirement for membership in
the Alabama Gang – to be nice to people.

Michael Waltrip

I've heard them boo just about everybody,
but they never booed Neil Bonnett.

Betty Carlan

I started Winston Cup racing in 1979 with
   guys like Buddy Baker, Bobby and Donnie
Allison and Cale Yarborough. I got beat a lot.
       But I also learned a lot.

Dale Earnhardt

You could give Buddy Baker an anvil
   in the morning, and he'd tear it up by noon.

Tiny Lund

When you beat a Petty,
   you have to beat the whole darn family.

Tiny Lund

I may share the title with him, but
Richard Petty will always be "The King."

Dale Earnhardt

I don't think anybody is going to be
the next Richard Petty.

Jeff Gordon

I figure Lee Petty is the greatest race driver
who ever lived.

Richard Petty

Darrell Waltrip is my kind of driver.

A.J. Foyt

I wouldn't take anything for my past.
I think I've had one of the most exciting lives
anybody could have lived.

Junior Johnson

Red Farmer is probably the only race driver
still going who's drawing Social Security.

Donnie Allison

I hope my boys make good in racing
'cause they'll starve to death if they don't.

George Elliott
Father of Bill, Ernie and Dan

My name can be a blessing or a curse,
depending on how well I run in a race.

Lake Speed

I was racing sprint cars long before
I had a driver's license.

Jeff Gordon

I talk to myself all the time in the car.

Rusty Wallace

The Drivers

He's a junkyard dog and I like him,
  although I get mad at him when
  he pushes people around.

Rick Hendrick on Dale Earnhardt

Catching Dale and passing him
  are two different things.

Bobby Labonte on Dale Earnhardt

Dale is the most determined driver
  in the world.

Richard Childress

Everything I've accomplished in my career
  I trace back to being taught
  by Ralph Earnhardt.

Dale Earnhardt

I raced Ralph for years and years, and Dale drives just like his Daddy.

Ned Jarrett

Once you've raced,
you never forget it and
you never get over it.

Richard Childress

4

Behind the Wall

A driver is nothing without equipment. Absent the right car and the right crew, even the most talented racer will soon be lapped.

Buddy Baker wryly noted, "Good equipment has a lot to do with how smart a driver you are." Baker understood that the thin line between winning and losing is more a matter of car than driver. Behind the pit wall, a winning crew must be organized, talented, and well-funded. Attention to detail is imperative. So is cooperation and hard work.

Standing behind every champion is a great crew. Buddy Baker said it, but all drivers know it: Racing is a team sport.

Three-fourths of a race is won in the garage.

Lee Petty

I'm a firm believer that it's
75% race car and 25% driver.

Kenny Schrader

I've seen many races won in the pit.

Glen Wood

Surround yourself with the best people.

Rusty Wallace

A second is a second, whether you pick it up on the track or in the pits – and most races are decided by less than a second.

Darrell Waltrip

If you look good, there's a reason – the crew.

Lake Speed

Listen to your pit crew.

Ralph Moody

It's my team that makes me look good.

Ward Burton

I don't feel I'm a step above anyone on this team. I'm just another link in the chain.

Jeff Gordon

Our strategy is based upon preparation.

Roger Penske

Preparation has a lot to do with luck.

Terry Labonte

What kind of plays do you think they
would have on Broadway
if they didn't have rehearsals?

Harry Hyde

I'll never be able to leave a car or engine alone.
Besides, I'm improving it.

Lee Petty

We never really get done with the car.
We just quit working on it for that week.

Robbie Loomis

The moment every engine builder waits for
is the testing of his new creation.

Waddell Wilson

Holman-Moody trained a lot of people:
Jake Elder, Dan Ford, Robert Yates, Jimmy
Tucker, Larry Wallace, a lot more.

Waddell Wilson

I learned that preventative maintenance was
as important to winning as a fast car.

Bobby Allison

Rick Hendrick got a little gasoline
in his veins and never got it out.

Darrell Waltrip

The one thing that's kept me in racing
all these years is the closeness
of the teams in the garage.

Junie Donlavey

Every time somebody says,
"What do you owe it to?" I say,
"I owe it to the pit crew."

Kyle Petty

Y ou can't be a loner and be a racer because
the cycle spins so fast – you can be on top
one day and right on the bottom the next.

Junie Donlavey

I t's not one area or another.
It's the whole team as a unit.

Davey Allison

I t takes the crew and the owner. Everybody
has got to want to win as bad as the driver.

Fred Lorenzen

To get to the Super Bowl, whether it's football
or auto racing, you've got to have a team.

Tim Richmond

A quarterback has to have blockers.
A singer has to have a band.
A pitcher needs eight other players.
They can't do it by themselves,
and neither can I.

Dale Earnhardt

We work together, we play together,
we win together, and we lose together.

Dale Earnhardt

There are three major factors in the car:
a good body, horsepower and a good chassis.

Todd Bodine

You want a car that goes through the air
like an arrow.

Waddell Wilson

If I've learned anything about racing,
it's that you can over-engineer and make
things worse by trying too many things.

Harry Gant

I can't afford new stuff, but the used parts
I buy from Benny Parsons are usually
as good as new.

J.D. McDuffie

5

Success

In racing, success seldom comes easy. The road to the top requires years of hard work, lots of natural talent and a pocket full of good luck. Even then, no guarantees exist.

Darrell Waltrip, no stranger to victory lane, said, "Success doesn't come from doing one thing right. Success comes from doing a lot of little things right."

The following advice comes from men who have earned their way into the record books by doing the little things right. Again and again and again.

If you don't charge from the start, there are
plenty of great drivers who will.

Cale Yarborough

My strategy?
Go out there and run wide open.

Charlie Glotzbach

You have to be a fierce competitor,
but you also have to learn to control yourself.

Richard Petty

There's a fine line between being confident
and being obnoxious.

Darrell Waltrip

I want to do it my way.
I don't mind the hard work and I enjoy the
challenge. If I succeed, I've done it myself.
If I fail, well, I can say I tried.

Alan Kulwicki

When you work all your life to get someplace,
you don't quit when you finally get there.

Ricky Craven

You're always learning.
    It's a great big process that takes
      a long time to figure out.

Rick Mast

I failed in 1982. But I came back,
    and my failure built character.

Mark Martin

If a man climbed the ladder of success
    without capitalizing on his mistakes,
      I don't know who he was.

Harry Hyde

What happened last week is over and
done with. We race one week and
go on to the next race.

Dale Earnhardt

No matter how good you're running –
or how bad you're running – finish the race.

Alan Kulwicki

It may be a struggle in the beginning,
but I've never had anything worthwhile
that I didn't work hard for.

Dick Brooks

You can make up for any lack of ability
with desire and heart.

Greg Sacks

I drive a race car 100 percent every race,
and that is what I intend to do until I retire.

Dale Earnhardt

I never cheated to win a race.
I always thought a man needed to win on
his ability, working on cars and driving ...
not because of cheating.

Red Farmer

Mr. Johnson, you don't know who I am,
but some day I'd sure like to drive for you.
Jimmy Spencer, age 22

15 years later, Spencer got his wish by becoming a driver
for Junior Johnson.

To me, the real heroes are people
who do worthwhile things without
the thought of monetary gain.
Benny Parsons

Success is being happy with yourself.
Kyle Petty

There's no reason
not to aim high.

Harry Gant

6

Advice

The Greek playwright Sophocles correctly observed, "No enemy is worse than bad advice." It follows that good advice is a dear friend indeed. The following good thoughts are submitted for your approval by notable racing legends. Read and heed.

Never tell your racing plans.
    You might need to use them again.
                                    Cale Yarborough

Never drive over your head.
                                    Tim Flock

Never settle for being anything but the best.
                                    A.J. Foyt

Never dwell on the crashes.
                                    Richard Petty

Never stop the educational process.

Alan Kulwicki

If you're gonna play with rattlesnakes,
   you better know what rattlesnakes do.

Smokey Yunick

There's no need to get nervous.
      If I got too nervous, I'd say
      I was in the wrong business.

David Pearson

You can't let outside things interfere.
      Racing is about being the coolest
         and the strongest.

Dale Earnhardt

Wipe away fear
like you wipe away
water from a windshield.

Cale Yarborough

First you learn to drive fast.
  Next, you learn to drive fast in traffic.
  Then, you learn how to do it for 500 miles.

Alan Kulwicki

The first thing you have to do
  is beat the race track.

Benny Parsons

First you learn to finish, then you learn to win.

Bill Elliott

My mother always told me,
"If you can't win, at least be second."

Darrell Waltrip

Stay out of trouble. The money is at
the end of the race, not the beginning.

Buck Baker

If you want to cash in, you've got to be there
when the man begins passing out the money.

Joe Weatherly

Avoid accidents.
You can't win any races in the hospital.

Fred Lorenzen

Advice

Have a back-up plan for everything
you can think of.

Humpy Wheeler

Don't pay too much attention to what
happened last week or last race.
Just look ahead and do better next time.

Richard Petty

Don't look backwards. Look to the next lap
and stand on it.

Fred Lorenzen

Son, if people don't like
you as who you are,
they sure won't like you
as who you try to be.

Father's Advice to Cale Yarborough

Work hard, be fair, and don't mess in other people's business.

Junior Johnson

7

Attitude

Racing places a premium on hope. For a great driver, optimism comes as standard equipment. How else could one persevere despite overwhelming odds and years of frustration?

Marcus Aurelius (no relation to Dave Marcis) was a great Roman emperor and philosopher. He wrote, "Our universe is change; our lives are what our thoughts make of it." Almost two thousand years later, Bill Elliott made a similar observation when he noted, "It's mind over matter. If you don't mind, it don't matter."

If life is getting you down, then it's time to make a pit stop for a quick attitude adjustment. After all, if you can't trust Marcus Aurelius and Bill Elliott, who can you trust?

Without a positive attitude, you're not
going anywhere – in racing or in life.

Brett Bodine

You can't allow yourself to think
about all the things that can go wrong.
You've got to concentrate on winning.

Grant Adcox

Whether it's in racing or in life,
so much of what we do depends on attitude.

Dick Trickle

If you don't have confidence in your ability,
who will – or should?

Lee Roy Yarbrough

If you don't believe, you don't belong.

Alan Kulwicki's Credo

In the kind of business we're in, you have
to have faith. Racing the way we do,
you put your life in God's hands.

Richard Petty

We must accept life as it goes along,
and do the best with the hand we've been
dealt. Our religious beliefs and the racing
fraternity helped Judy and me.

Bobby Allison

Conviction is a belief you hold ...
and it holds you.

Bobby Allison

When today's race is over, it's over.
The only race that matters
is the one coming up.

Harry Gant

I just keep pluggin'. I haven't won yet,
but I might next week.

J.D. McDuffie

Always have a next great goal.

Alan Kulwicki

There's an attitude that comes
        from being a winner.

Richard Petty

I guess I learn something from
        every driver and every race.

David Pearson

It's a never-ending cycle. Racing keeps
    changing and we've got to keep learning.

Hut Stricklin

Do the best you can.
    But don't go crazy with the pressure.

Ray Evernham

I've always been enthusiastic ...
     enthusiastic enough to be optimistic.
                                        Bobby Allison

The mental aspect of racing makes you
          more tired than the physical.
                                        Richard Petty

Most pressure is self-inflicted pressure.
                                        Jimmy Hensley

Enthusiasm finds opportunities and energy makes the most of them.

Buddy Parrott

8

Hard Charging

Cale Yarborough earned a reputation for running flat-out. He once commented, "There are two kinds of racers: the hard-chargers and also-rans." Yarborough understood that stock car racing is not for the passive or the faint of heart.

Winning drivers learn to balance aggression with discretion. On the track, recklessness pays no dividends, but neither does timidity. Consequently, the best drivers learn when to charge and when to save the equipment.

Darrell Waltrip summed it up when he said, "On the short tracks, you've got to go into the corner second and come out first." Spoken like a true hard-charger.

The definition of racing:
Green means go, checkered means stop,
and no holds barred in between.
Richard Petty

In racing, there is no rest between plays,
no substitutions. You can't let
down for a minute.
Cale Yarborough

Tough competition helped me. Nobody ever
gets better if he isn't challenged.
Richard Petty

It's every man for himself on the last lap.
You take no prisoners on the last lap.
Sterling Marlin

Stock Car Wisdom

There aren't any new frontiers anymore,
not even the moon. The only thing left
for these guys is to go a little deeper
into that first turn.

Ken Squier

When rocks are hitting the fender and the
wall's coming, you know you went in too hard.

Darrell Waltrip

A wreck can knock the cockiness out of you.

Fred Lorenzen

Anybody who breaks only one or two bones
per season is lucky.

Ricky Rudd

You can't race hard and drive dumb.
And you can't race smart and not drive hard.

Ted Musgrave

I'd just like to be remembered as a man who
drove every lap just as hard as he could.

Cale Yarborough

If she runs right, run her hard.
    If she don't, back off.

Lee Petty

When we raced against each other, Daddy
didn't give me any special consideration.
I was just another car to him, and he would
just as soon beat me up as a total stranger.

Richard Petty

I've never wanted to hurt somebody
because they did something to me. You want
to protect yourself, but not kill somebody.

Dale Earnhardt

In the race, you have to know
    when to charge and when to hold back.
        You have to feel it.

Richard Petty

I drive by the seat of my pants, and what
    goes through the seat goes into my mind
        and tells me what to do next.

Ernie Irvan

On the track, you may get mad,
    but you know you're going to see
    each other next weekend. You have
    to find a way to work it out.

Mark Martin

Running bumper-to-bumper with a guy,
    wide-open ... that's total commitment.

Cale Yarborough

When the car's running right,
> you're in your own little world.
> You're almost a part of the machinery.

Buddy Baker

The safest place to be is out front – flat out.

Dale Earnhardt

The only way to watch the other guys
> is out front. You don't have to worry
> about what anyone else is doing.

Junior Johnson

Sometimes you've got to do
> a little mirror driving to win.

Sterling Marlin

People remember who wins
> on the super speedways.

Jimmy Spencer

Never initiate.
Retaliate.

Bobby Allison

I never hit anybody out of malice or recklessness ... unless they bump me twice.

Tim Flock

9

That's Racing

The Talmud proclaims, "In business, everything depends upon aid from heaven." The same could be said about racing. Skill plays a part in every race – so does equipment. But fate also has a role to play.

Drivers learn that racing luck is as much a part of the sport as pit stops. On the track, countless things can go wrong: Engines blow, so do tires. Sometimes, accidents are unavoidable, and sometimes, no one is to blame.

Every trip to victory lane requires talent and preparation, but it also demands a heaping helping of good luck. That's the nature of the human condition. And, that's racing.

The bull stops when the green flag drops.

Racing Saying

During a race you have no idea how many
times cars *almost* crash.

Richard Petty

This is a real humbling sport.
It can knock you down real quick.

Ernie Irvan

Racing is not kind to you a lot.
The times it is kind to you are
what make it so special.

Dave Mader, III

This is still a down-homesey, folksy, blue-collar, Middle American sport. We just never have gotten too big for our britches.

Darrell Waltrip

I like the money and I like the fame, but if I were a millionaire and we raced in private, I'd still be racing.

Cale Yarborough

Road racing is like getting to run around the back roads around your house, but you don't have to worry about the cops.

Hut Stricklin

Driving a race car is like dancing with a chain saw.

Cale Yarborough

If a man has to run you into the wall
to beat you, that ain't racing.

Bill Elliott

In the old days, I thought it was easier
to knock them out of the way
than it was to race with them.

Buddy Baker

Rubbin' to get by somebody if they're
pinching you down – that's not rough.
That's racin'.

Dale Earnhardt

During a crash, you're too busy to be scared.

Lee Roy Yarbrough

I'm getting a little tired
of my new job
with NASCAR:
Chief Wall Tester.

Marty Robbins

It's a chess game on wheels,
and you better play it smart.

Harry Gant

Part is driving. Part is preparation.
But the biggest part is luck.

Bill Elliott

Racers don't like to talk about bad luck.

Richard Petty

You may have a powerful motor, but you've
got to get through the turns to use it.

Richard Petty

Tires make the difference between tenth
and first – and that's a lot of difference.

Junior Johnson

Everything you try to make the car do
depends on those four little spots
where the tires touch.

Harry Gant

It's all in the tires.

Darrell Waltrip

There are thousands of ways to lose a race.
David Pearson

I was doing plenty wrong,
but they done wronger.
Richard Petty
After winning the Nashville 400

Just go for the gusto
and see how things work out.
Alan Kulwicki

Racing is a mystery.
It can't be taught
or written down
or even told.

Cale Yarborough

The best way to make a small fortune in racing is to start with a big one.

Junior Johnson

<u>10</u>

Hard Work

When young Richard Petty was beginning his career, father Lee took his boy aside and gave this advice: "If you expect to make it in anything, you better put all you've got into it. I don't care if you're a clown or if you're selling pots and pans, you have to work a little harder than the next guy."

As Ben Franklin once said, "Diligence makes good luck." Both Ben and Lee were right: hard work does pay dividends, whether you're a clown or The King.

Hard Work

My father was a mechanical genius
who could do more with less than anybody
I've ever seen. He taught us to work.

Franklin Scott

Son of Wendall Scott, the first African-American to successfully
compete in NASCAR Grand National Racing.

The longer and harder you work
for something, the more you appreciate it.

Alan Kulwicki

You're not going to win
unless you've done your homework.

Bill Elliott

We're not lucky.
We win because we work hard.

Roger Penske

I believe in fate and luck, but it helps
if you're working at something you love.
Rick Hendrick

The good Lord directs some of us,
and I consider it a privilege to have found
what I really wanted to do at an early age.
Humpy Wheeler

Nothing comes easy in racing,
but when you're on top, all the
struggles seem worthwhile.
Joe Weatherly

You never really know anybody
until you work with them.

Morgan Shepherd

Why did I take up racing?
I was too lazy to work and too chicken to
steal.

Tim Richmond

Unless you win 31 races,
you can improve on what you did last year.

Jimmy Spencer

Do it right. Make every race and
　　　run for the championship.

Richard Petty

When a fellow wins a race or finishes
　　　among the leaders, you know
　　　somebody has been working hard.

Lee Petty

When the season is over,
　　　I'll have a nervous breakdown.
　　　I would already have had one,
　　　but I haven't had the time.

Bill Elliott

Whoever said,
"There's no rest for the
weary," must have been
a stock car mechanic.

Glen Wood

11

Adversity

In *As You Like It*, Shakespeare wrote,

"Sweet are the uses of adversity,
Which, like the toad, ugly and venomous,
Wears yet a precious jewel in his head."

According to Will, a race track must be a very sweet place indeed, because adversity, it seems, is everywhere.

Over the years, drivers have been tested by the slings and arrows of outrageous fortune. For pioneering drivers, financial hardship was the rule, not the exception. Even today, drivers face the specter of serious injury, or worse. Still they persevere.

Seneca observed, "Fire is the test of gold; adversity the test of strong men." Here's what some strong men have to say about their own tough times.

I've learned by trial and error.
I've got a master's degree
in the school of hard knocks.

Cale Yarborough

Auto racing is probably the toughest sport
to get a start in. In other sports,
you can show your talent on your own.
In racing, so much needs to jell before
a driver can showcase his talents.

Ned Jarrett

There's a lot of work and heartache
to make it from the bottom to the top.

David Pearson

Nothing comes easy to anyone in racing.

Joe Weatherly

B asically, my philosophy is to keep working
and keep trying. It'll all eventually work out.
If it doesn't, so what? You've got to be
doing something anyhow.

Dave Marcis

I 've been around a long time,
 and I know you just got to keep going.
 Just lay your ears back and go at it.

Sterling Marlin

I f a team can make it through the ups and
 downs to win two or three races a year,
 they've had a good season.
 I'll say that until I quit racing.

Bill Elliott

Each championship is different,
    but one thing stays the same.
    You've got to do it race by race.

Dale Earnhardt

My mind is not on how well the season's
    going, but on how to make it better.

Jeff Gordon

When you have consistency,
    everything begins to take care of itself.

Jimmy Hensley

Never let a crash dim your enthusiasm.
Heck, we all have days like that.

Richard Petty

The value of making mistakes
is to remember each one and to try
not to make it again.

Harry Hyde

You've got to have some breaks, but you've
got to make some of your own breaks, too.

Jeremy Mayfield

Winston Cup racing is very humbling.
The problem is everybody is so good.
You've got to be working or striving
or you're always getting behind.

Rick Mast

Your head never begins to swell
until your mind stops growing.

Alan Kulwicki

Tough times are the Lord's way of teaching me to be strong.

Geoff Bodine

On the way to the top,
you've got to eat a lot
of dirt and hope to get
a break before
you get killed.

David Pearson

You win some.
You lose some.
You wreck some.

Dale Earnhardt

12

The Tracks

Every race track, like every race driver, has a unique personality. What follows are notable quotes by notable racers about notable tracks.

Talladega is the only place where
we finish closer than we start.

Terry Labonte

No one ever won at Talladega
by driving conservatively.

Grant Adcox

Talladega is like playing chess
at 200 miles per hour.

Neil Bonnett

Eula Faye, pass the potatoes, please.
Sterling's running at Talladega.

Coo Coo Marlin

His way of telling Sterling's mother about their son's
first race at the superspeedway

Daytona is our Super Bowl and Kentucky
Derby. If you win this race,
you've already had a good season.

Richard Petty

Daytona has brought racing up
to the standard it is today. The whole sport
has grown around the Daytona Speedway.

Lee Petty

At Daytona, the weather makes it feel like
someone has gone around the track with
a can of oil. The car slips and slides a lot.

Ted Musgrave

Bill France was the smartest man
I ever met, and that includes three presidents
of the United States.

Clyde Bolton

Rockingham will test you at every turn.
Darrell Waltrip

Five hundred miles at Rockingham is the
toughest test there is for a man or a car.
Lee Roy Yarbrough

Martinsville Speedway always has been
my baby doll, and we'll always
keep her beautiful.
Clay Earles

Bristol is my favorite short track.
Rusty Wallace

I've always wished my daddy could have
    raced Charlotte in a competitive car.
                                    Dale Earnhardt

A lot can happen at Pocono.
    We've had dogs, turkeys, and about
    everything imaginable on the track.
                                    Doyle Ford

I like Pocono. I almost got killed there
    last year, but I still like it.
                                    Neil Bonnett

Darlington, to me, is the greatest race track
in the world. Darlington lets you know
if you're a driver or not.

Fred Lorenzen

At Darlington, you don't race the other drivers.
You run against the track.

Richard Petty

Same ol' Darlington. They can make it
smoother, but you still drive the
same number of inches off the walls.

David Pearson

Darlington is tough. The third turn
got me again, but this time I took out Dad, too.
That really hurt.

Davey Allison

I'd rather run on any other track than Darlington, but I'd rather win at Darlington than any other track.

Bobby Isaac

I grew up thinking that the Southern 500 was about as important as the World Series, the Kentucky Derby, and the Indianapolis 500, all wrapped up into one.

Richard Petty

13

Danger

In stock car racing, danger lurks everywhere. Despite countless safety measures, a race car can still be hazardous to one's health.

Fireball Roberts said, "In a race, I'm always scared, but what I fear most is fire." In 1964, Roberts was caught up in a flaming crash at Darlington. He later died from his burns.

Mark Twain correctly observed that courage is not the absence of fear, but the resistance to fear. Twain understood that some men, like Fireball Roberts, seem compelled to face and conquer their inner demons. When these heroes enter the arena, the rest of us can only stand and marvel.

I'm doing what I like best. This is my life, and I'm having too much fun to retire now.

Tiny Lund

9 days before he died in a crash at Talladega.

If racing were completely safe, everyone would do it, and it wouldn't be a sport.

Tim Flock

If the lion didn't bite the tamer every once in a while, it wouldn't be exciting.

Darrell Waltrip

Racing is dangerous, but I've been in lots worse situations as a pipe fitter.

Neil Bonnett

I'd rather die at the race track than die of cancer.

A. J. Foyt

I look at it this way:
when it's your time to go,
you're going.

David Pearson

Danger

I'm more nervous watching from the pits
than I ever was driving.

Lee Petty

Watching from the booth, the danger is
obvious. Looking through the windshield,
it's not.

Benny Parsons

There's no bigger surprise than
to be tooling along at 200 and suddenly
getting hit from the rear.

Darrell Waltrip

The Lord works miracles. He did one
yesterday in front of 35,000 people.

Michael Waltrip

After his grinding crash at Bristol in 1990.

The week of Daytona 1988 had to be
my greatest accomplishment.
Maybe I'll remember it some day.
Bobby Allison

Fireball was sort of my idol growing up.
When he got killed, it sort of took the racing
spirit out of me, like when you
finally find out about Santa Claus.
Fred Lorenzen

When you start thinking too much about
wrecks and high speeds, it's time to quit.
Glen Wood

Death and injury are a part of this sport.
But not as big a part as some people think.
A. J. Foyt

I feel safer on a racetrack
than I do on Houston's expressways.
A.J. Foyt

You can't live your life
in fear of what's
gonna happen next.

Buddy Baker

14

Winning and Losing

In 1959, Richard Petty thought he had won his first race until a protest was lodged – by his own father! After the scorecards were checked, Lee was declared the winner. The elder Petty said simply, "When he wins, the boy can have it, but he ain't gonna have it give to him."

Drivers take winning and losing *very* seriously. Here are some words of wisdom from men who have experienced their share of both.

You're out there to win,
   not to bring your car home in one piece.
                                    Richard Petty

There's no second, third or fourth.
         Either you win, or you lose.
                                    Cale Yarborough

You can run a good race and finish second,
      but it's only a great race if you win.
                                    Geoff Bodine

It's 31 races a year and you've got to believe
that you're going to win them all.
Not one, not two. Every single one.

Dale Earnhardt

I'd be lying if I said the money didn't matter,
but the best thing about the championship is
that it can never be taken away.
It's yours, and that's that.

Alan Kulwicki

Any good winner is a bad loser.

Bobby Allison

As long as you're winning, why quit?

Red Farmer

No one wants to quit when he's losing, and no one wants to quit when he's winning.

Richard Petty

I'm determined to stick around till I win one. That means I'll be driving forever.

Marty Robbins

The best you can do on any given day
is put yourself in a position to win. After that,
if the circumstances are right, you'll win.

Richard Petty

Look for ways to win,
rather than expecting something to happen
that will make you lose.

Billy Wade

Sometimes you have to lose
before you can learn how to win.

Dale Earnhardt

In this business, experience is
more important than muscle.

Lee Petty

You love to win, but you hate to win
due to someone else's misfortune.
Junie Donlavey

You have to be philosophical about racing
because you can't run strong at every track.
Richard Petty

My luck was better than Richard's.
I had greater luck rather than greater skill.
Joe Weatherly
Upon winning the title in 1963.

Sometimes, you win by
being the best of what's left.
Bill Elliott

Winners never quit and quitters never win.
It's true in life. It's true on the track.

Bill France, Sr.

Let your right foot do the talking.

Tim Richmond

The first big win for any driver is so important.
When it finally happens, it's Utopia.

Harry Hyde

That's why I took an extra lap – so I could
wipe away the tears.

Jeff Gordon

After winning the inaugural Brickyard 400.

The purpose of a race is to run
the car as fast as it will go and win.
With that in mind, we went racing.

David Pearson

I'm not going to do anything to harm anybody,
but I'll do anything to win.

Dale Earnhardt

Win on Sunday, sell on Monday.

Bob Tripolsky

Pontiac spokesman commenting on
victories and showroom sales.

As good as racing can be,
you're never immune from the heartache.

Cale Yarborough

My motherly instincts tell me I should pull
for Davey. But I have to pull for Bobby
because he still pays the bills.

Judy Allison

When her son, Davey, and her husband, Bobby,
clashed head-to-head in a Daytona 500 qualifying race.

Hut and Davey went down to the wire.
I wasn't sure who to pull for,
my driver or my son.

Bobby Allison

Following a Davey Allison / Hut Stricklin 1-2 finish.

It's not the fastest car that wins the race;
it's the quickest one.

Lee Petty

I led the lap I wanted to – the last one.

Joe Weatherly

After coming back from 4 laps down
to win the National 400 in 1962.

15

Observations

We conclude with assorted thoughts on a wide range of topics. Enjoy.

You can turn a driver into a media person,
but you can't do the opposite.

Richard Childress

There are probably guys out here walking
the street who could win with a good car.

Harry Hyde

Show me a guy that's got a heavy
pocketbook, and it'll drag him down in speed.

Junior Johnson

What does it take to be a great driver? Ability, determination, guts, and a heavy foot.

A. J. Foyt

Race fans are the most dedicated
in all of sports. Heck, sometimes
they even fight for you.

Richard Petty

Without the fans, I'm nothing.

Bill Elliott

To me, every time I sign an autograph,
it's just like giving somebody a Christmas gift.

Richard Petty

We're in the entertainment business.

Bill France, Jr.

Make the fans comfortable, give them a good show, and give them their money's worth.

Clay Earles

The fun of racing? No question. It's the people. That's the real fun of racing.

Junie Donlavey

Petty likes Dentyne. Pearson likes Spearmint. Cale likes Beechnut. Some of 'em I give Teaberry, too. I tell 'em if they want to drive funny today, I'll give 'em Teaberry.

Red Robinson

Robinson earned his reputation as the fan who gave gum to drivers before each race.

I'm superstitious.
I never go to Victory Lane until it's over.
Rick Hendrick

If the Good Lord ever wanted to help out
an independent, this was his chance.
Dave Marcis
After his victory in the Richmond 400

I got out about the time the money got in.
Coo Coo Marlin

I didn't miss out on a family life because
of racing. I had one because of it.

Richard Petty

My daddy was a race driver so I became
a race driver. If he had been a grocer,
I might have been a grocer, too.

Richard Petty

Growing up in racing gave me a lot of
advantages in understanding the sport, but it
didn't prepare me for being a driver's wife.

Pam Allison Stricklin

Daughter of Donnie Allison, wife of Hut Stricklin

I raised four boys – three sons
and my husband, David.

Helen Pearson

A race car doesn't know
how old the driver is.

Bobby Allison

In the early days, the fans got into
the moonshine. Sometimes it looked
like a riot starting.

Bob Latford

Publicist for Charlotte Motor Speedway

If you don't like this party, there's always
another one startin' in five minutes.

Curtis Turner

Some decisions shouldn't be made
on an empty stomach.

Dale Earnhardt

I used to like the St. Louis Cardinals
because I lived in St. Louis, but I can't cheer
for them now. Wrong brewery.

Rusty Wallace

Everybody has their own opinions.
That's what makes racing so much fun.

Buddy Baker

Plowin' a garden with a mule is the best way you can plow a garden.

Junior Johnson

For good luck I've tried chicken wishbones, turkey wishbones, and rabbits' feet. I find that chicken wishbones work best.

Joe Weatherly

Stock car racing is the most exciting sport in the world.

Richard Petty

Sources

Notes

Notes

Notes

Notes

Notes

Notes

About the Author

Criswell Freeman is a Doctor of Clinical Psychology living in Nashville, Tennessee. He is the author of *When Life Throws You a Curveball, Hit It* and *The Wisdom Series* from WALNUT GROVE PRESS. He is also a published country music songwriter.

About Wisdom Books

Wisdom Books chronicle memorable quotations in an easy-to-read style. Written by Criswell Freeman, this series provides inspiring, thoughtful and humorous messages from entertainers, athletes, scientists, politicians, clerics, writers and renegades. Each title focuses on a particular region or special interest.

Combining his passion for quotations with extensive training in psychology, Dr. Freeman revisits timeless themes such as perseverance, courage, love, forgiveness and faith.

"Quotations help us remember the simple yet profound truths that give life perspective and meaning," notes Freeman. "When it comes to life's most important lessons, we can all use gentle reminders."

The Wisdom Series
by Dr. Criswell Freeman

Wisdom Made In America
ISBN 1-887655-07-7

The Book of Southern Wisdom
ISBN 0-9640955-3-X

The Book of Country Music Wisdom
ISBN 0-9640955-1-3

The Golfer's Book of Wisdom
ISBN 0-9640955-6-4

The Wisdom of Southern Football
ISBN 0-9640955-7-2

The Book of Texas Wisdom
ISBN 0-9640955-8-0

The Book of Florida Wisdom
ISBN 0-9640955-9-9

The Book of Stock Car Wisdom
ISBN 1-887655-12-3

The Wisdom of Old-Time Baseball
ISBN 1-887655-08-5

Wisdom Books are available through
booksellers everywhere. For information about
a retailer near you, call 1-800-256-8584.